Start
Reading 5

Derek Strange

OXFORD UNIVERSITY PRESS

Kimau's paper bag

1 Kimau and Makula walked quickly beside the brown African river, the Tana River, with its crocodiles and its hippopotamuses. They were a long

5 way from their camp, and it was late. *They* could already see the moon and the stars in the sky. They could hear the lions and other wild animals near the path, in the long brown grass and

10 the small trees. The noises of the animals made the two boys walk faster and faster. They were in a hurry now.

'We must get back to the camp

15 quickly,' Kimau said. *He* was frightened.

'Sh! We must be as quiet as we can, too. The lions are hunting for food . . .' Makula suddenly stopped and held up

20 one hand. 'Listen!'

They listened.

'An elephant!' Makula whispered.

They walked as quietly as they could along the path, and stopped behind a

25 big tree. There was a large elephant twenty metres in front of them on the path.

'Don't let it hear us!' Makula whispered.

30 Suddenly the elephant turned. It could hear them and smell them, too. *It* put its long trunk up into the air. (Elephants cannot see very well, but they can hear well with their big ears

35 and they can smell well with their long trunks.)

The boys hid behind the tree and did not move.

Slowly the elephant came towards

40 them. Then it stopped, only five or six metres away from their tree. *It* screamed loudly and angrily, and waved its ears backwards and forwards.

45 'It's going to attack us!' whispered Makula.

'We must do something . . .' answered Kimau, and he pulled a big brown paper bag from his pocket.

50 There were some sweets in the bag. *He* let the sweets fall into the long grass and he started to blow into the bag quickly.

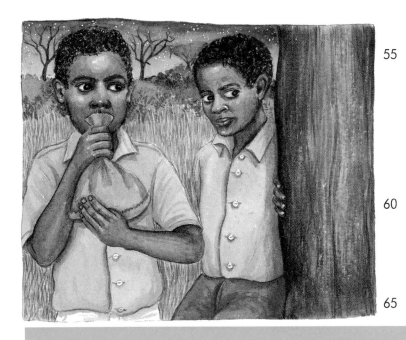

55 Then he hit the bag hard with his hand:

BANG

It made a very loud noise, like a gun.

The elephant stopped. It stood and listened. Then it screamed angrily again 60 and started to turn away. It ran through the grass and its big strong legs broke the branches of the small trees.

'Come on, Makula! Quick!' shouted Kimau, and the two boys ran back to 65 the camp as fast as they could.

Exercises

A True or false?

1 There are crocodiles and hippo-potamuses in the Tana River.

2 Kimau and Makula met an angry lion near the river.

3 There was an elephant on the path in front of the boys.

4 The elephant could hear and smell Kimau and Makula.

5 The elephant was angry and it started to attack the boys.

6 The noise of Kimau's paper bag frightened the elephant away.

B Read again. Answer the questions.

1 (Line 6) 'They could already see the moon . . .' Who are they?

2 (Line 15) 'He was frightened.' Who is he?

3 (Line 21) 'They listened.' Who are they?

4 (Line 32) 'It put . . .' What is it?

5 (Line 41) 'It screamed loudly . . .' What is it?

6 (Line 51) 'He let the sweets fall . . .' Who is he?

C Finish the words.
Match the words with the pictures.

1 H __ P P __ P __ T __ M __ S

2 C R __ C __ D __ L __

3 L __ __ N

4 __ L __ P H __ N T

3

1 In the north of Thailand, on the side of a mountain, there is a small village. Its name is Huey Khan. The village is in the middle of a large, beautiful forest. For hundreds of years Huey Khan has been a quiet, happy place.

2 Dawania Jinjao was born in the village. She has lived there with her family all her life. She is now thirteen years old. She loves the village and the forest around it. She has always played in the forest with her friends. Together they have climbed the trees and they have watched the animals and the birds. Together they have chased butterflies and they have listened to the tigers in the forest at night.

3 But life in Huey Khan has changed. Hundreds of men from two big companies have arrived with chain-saws and tractors, and they have started to cut down the tall, old trees. The men have cut down more than 3,000 hectares of the forest near the village. The tractors have pulled the logs down the mountain to the valley, and lorries have carried the logs away. After only six months the forest at Huey Khan has started to disappear. Dawania cannot play there with her friends any more.

4 The village people have become very angry. They have decided to fight the companies. They want to stop the men and save their forest. Without the trees, the rain is now washing all the good earth down the mountain into the river. New trees cannot grow. Already the animals, the birds and the butterflies have moved away to other mountains, away from the noise of the men with tractors and saws. The mountain at Huey Khan is becoming a desert.

Exercises

A Answer the questions.

1 Where is the village of Huey Khan?

2 Who has always played in the forest near the village?

3 Who has arrived in the village of Huey Khan?

4 What have the men done in the forest near the village?

5 What have the people of Huey Khan decided to do?

6 Where have all the animals, birds and butterflies gone?

B Match the sentences with the paragraphs. Write the numbers.

The people of Huey Khan want to stop the men and save their forest.	4
Dawania and the other children of the village have always played in the forest near the village.	
Huey Khan has always been a quiet village in the middle of the forests in Thailand.	
Now things have changed in Huey Khan. Men from big companies have arrived and they are cutting down all the trees.	

C Find words.

```
a f t r e e r a
m o u n t a i n
i r l o g r v i
d e s e r t e m
k s t n n h r a
s t b i r d r l
```

On top of the world

Junko Tabei is a small, strong woman. She has short, black hair and a bright, smiling face. She lives with her family near Tokyo, in Japan.

Junko was the first woman to climb to the top of the highest mountain in the world, Mount Everest. She reached the summit of Everest on 16th May, 1975.

Here are some pages from her expedition diary:

14th May
        We have already walked more than a hundred kilometres. Now we are at 7,500 metres. The Sherpas are strong, brave people – they have carried our tents, our food and our oxygen to this camp. Tomorrow ten of us will move up to Base Camp, our last camp, at 8,500 metres.
        It is already difficult to breathe here – the air is very thin. Tomorrow we will need oxygen for our climb. The weather has been very good. I can see all the shining mountain tops across Nepal to India and to China.

15th May
        We have climbed 1,000 metres today and we are now at Base Camp. This is our last camp and tomorrow we will climb to the summit. There are ten of us here, but only four of us will try to reach the top tomorrow. No women have ever climbed as high as this on Mount Everest! We are the first! We have had good weather again today. We are very lucky.

16th May

Four of us started from Base Camp at four o'clock this morning. Yuri and Miwa climbed together and I was with Sherpa Anking Norgay.

After three hours, Yuri and Miwa stopped. They could not go higher. I went on with Sherpa Anking Norgay and after five hours we stood on top of the world!... But I have never been as tired as I am now.

Now we are safely back at Base Camp and I have just had a very long sleep. I feel strong again and I am very happy. This has been a very exciting day for me. I have reached the summit of the greatest mountain in the world, Everest!

Exercises

A Answer the questions.

1 How many people went to the expedition's Base Camp?
2 How high up the mountain was the Base Camp?
3 How many climbers from the expedition tried to climb to the summit?
4 At what time did they start to climb from Base Camp to the summit?
5 On what date did Junko Tabei reach the summit of Mount Everest?

B Put the sentences in order.

☐ After eight hours Junko Tabei became the first woman to stand on the top of Mount Everest.

1 The climbers and the Sherpas walked for more than 100 kilometres to reach the mountain.

☐ On 16th May 1975 four climbers started to climb very early in the morning.

☐ Ten climbers went up to their Base Camp on 15th May 1975.

☐ After three hours two of the other climbers stopped.

C Write the words in the squares.

1 They had good ..... on 14th and 15th May.
2 On 15th May they climbed 1,000 ..... to Base Camp.
3 They stood on the ..... after eight hours.
4 The Sherpas carried their food, ... and oxygen.
5 Mount ..... is the highest mountain in the world.

Lake Dawn Holiday Camp

Do you enjoy sport?
　　Come swimming and sailing with us at Lake Dawn!

Do you like excitement and danger?
　　Come rock-climbing, canoeing and horse-riding at Lake Dawn!

Computer programming? Cooking? Chess?
　　Choose your favorite hobbies and sports, and come on holiday with us at Lake Dawn!

Lake Dawn

What will you do every day at our Lake Dawn Holiday Camp?

Breakfast

Start the day with a big American breakfast at the Lake Dawn Diner at eight o'clock.

Morning

Meet us at the beach at nine. There's a good wind. The sun's shining. It's a great day to go sailing on the lake . . . or canoeing or fishing. You can choose. Our instructors are ready to help you. Later let's go back to the pool and go swimming. Our instructors are there, too.

Lunch-time

Are you hungry again? The Diner has burgers, pizzas, salads, ice-creams, fruit – all your favorite food, and as much as you can eat!

The Quiet Hour

Video time! Cartoons in the film theater. Or would you like an hour of computer programming in the computer room? Our instructors will help you to write your own programs in BASIC on one of the twenty 'Apple' computers there.

Or do you want to read your book quietly by the pool? You can do that, too.

Afternoon

What next? Horse-riding or rock-climbing beside the lake? Again, the instructors are ready, so let's go!

Or do you want to do some cooking in the 'Cookhouse'? There's everything there – you can make your own cakes, pies and cookies.

Evening

There's a barbecue down on the beach or donuts in the Diner. There's singing round the fire and dancing at the Lake Dawn Disco. Would you enjoy playing a quiet game of chess more? Choose anything . . . and have a good time!

Do you want to know more? Are you ready to join us? Write now! We are at:

Lake Dawn Holiday Camp Inc.
P.O. Box 1494 – BR,
Snake River, Colorado 85385.

Exercises

A True or false?

1 You can go swimming in the pool at Lake Dawn.
2 Some people enjoy fishing by the lake near the camp.
3 Instructors at the camp teach chess.
4 The 'Lake Dawn Diner' is the camp's restaurant.
5 'BASIC' is the name of a cartoon film.

B Answer the questions.

1 What is the address of the Lake Dawn Holiday Camp?
2 Which country is it in?
3 What can you have for breakfast at the Lake Dawn Diner?
4 What can you have for lunch at the Diner?
5 What do people usually do in the 'Cookhouse'?

C Which of these things do you do outside? Which do you do inside? Write the words in the boxes.

sailing
cooking
watching videos
rock-climbing
fishing
computer programming

horse-riding
playing chess
canoeing
dancing

Outside:	Inside:
sailing	

Kidnap!

1

Steve: Listen to this, Doug. 'Lisa Angelo is in town.'

Doug: Lisa Angelo? She's the American singer, isn't she?

Steve: That's right. And look – she's staying at this hotel, too! I would like to see her here. Her records are great.

Doug: Hey, look, Steve. That's her over there, isn't it? The woman in the white coat.

Steve: Yes, it is! That must be her Rolls Royce.

2

Steve: There's Lisa Angelo again, Doug . . . and there are those two men again.

Doug: She's in a hurry, isn't she? And the two men are following her, aren't they?

Steve: Why isn't she waiting for her car? Where is her car?

Doug: I don't know. Let's follow her, Steve. Perhaps she's in trouble . . .?

3

Doug: Look, Steve. Those two men are watching her, aren't they?

Steve: Yes, I think they are. She's stopped to look at the number of that house, and they've stopped behind her, too.

Doug: They're getting out of the car. I think they're going to kidnap her!

4

Steve: You're right. They're trying to make her get into the car with them.

Doug: She looks frightened, doesn't she?

Steve: Yes. Let's help her. We can stop those men! Come on!

5

Steve: I've caught you now, my friend.

Lisa: Oh, thank you! You're not police officers, are you?

Doug: No, we're not. We came to help you because we saw those two men following you. They wanted to kidnap you, didn't they?

Lisa: Yes, they did. I don't know why.

6

Lisa: I decided to walk to the studio because my car was late. It wasn't outside the restaurant. Suddenly these two men tried to push me into their car. They tried to kidnap me. But then these two young men came to help me because I was in trouble. The kidnappers let me go and started to run away . . .

Steve: But we stopped them, officer.

Doug: And then your men arrived to help us.

Officer: Well, you were very brave. Well done.

Lisa: And thank you!

Exercises

A Put the sentences in order.

- [ ] Lisa left the restaurant and started to walk to the studio.
- [1] Doug and Steve saw Lisa Angelo, the singer, at their hotel.
- [ ] Doug and Steve saved Lisa and caught the two kidnappers.
- [ ] Two men tried to make Lisa get into a black car with them.
- [ ] Lisa looked frightened.
- [ ] Lisa left the hotel and went to a restaurant in her Rolls Royce.

B Read and match.

1 Lisa Angelo is a famous singer, ... aren't they?

2 That's her Rolls Royce over there, ... doesn't she?

3 Those two men are following her, ... weren't they?

4 You're not police officers, ... isn't it?

5 She looks frightened, ... isn't she?

6 The two men were kidnappers, ... are you?

Day 350

Eleven months and sixteen days from Moon Station 'G' to this small, flat planet: Calulia. We have landed near a yellow lake that has a large square island in the middle of it. From here, the island looks golden. When we landed, the 'Sky Bird' made no wind and there was no dust. The ground here, which is white, is very hard. It is white rock.

We waited inside the 'Sky Bird' for three hours and watched the lake and the island carefully. Nothing moved. When we listened through the outside microphones, we heard nothing. Is there any life on Calulia? Even the yellow lake is calm and flat, with no waves.

Day 351

Today Captain Wells and I got into the space tractor and we left the spaceship. Doctor Nixon, who stayed with the others inside the 'Bird', watched us using the outside cameras.

When we got outside, we cut two small pieces from the ground near the 'Bird' and then we drove to the yellow lake. We took three small jars of the thick yellow liquid from the lake, which is as thick as oil or honey.

Day 352

After breakfast we put the skis on the tractor and I crossed over the yellow liquid of the lake with Captain Wells. The tractor moved very slowly over the lake towards the island. We first went round the island but we saw nothing moving. The island is square, with straight sides. We landed near one corner of it and we climbed up the side with our ropes to the top. The top is almost flat. Again we cut two pieces from the ground of the island. We wanted to look at it in the laboratory. It is very soft. We could not walk across it easily.

On the top of the island there were no buildings and we saw nothing moving. Captain Wells, who had her small video camera with her, wanted to go back to the space tractor and get some more film for it. I stayed on the top of the island for twenty minutes. But something went wrong.

Captain Wells did not come back. After twenty minutes I began to worry. I decided to look for her.

I went back to the space tractor, which was still at the corner of the island, but I could not see Captain Wells. I tried to contact her on my radio, but she did not answer. I tried to radio back to the 'Sky Bird', but again there was no answer. Was my radio broken? I decided to take the tractor and go round the island again. I tried to find Captain Wells. . . but I could not find her.

Day 353

I am very worried now. Yesterday I decided to come back to the 'Sky Bird' for a new radio and to get help from Doctor Nixon. When I reached the 'Bird', I found all the doors of the ship open. There was no one on the ship. It was empty.

Day 355

I have waited now for two days and I have watched the video screens all the time. I have not seen Captain Wells, Doctor Nixon or any of the others again. There has been no sound. Calulia is quiet and I am alone. . . Or am I? Is somebody here? Are they watching me? Are they waiting?

Exercises

A Answer the questions.

1 How long was the spaceship's journey from the Moon to Calulia?
2 Who went outside the spaceship on their second day on Calulia? (Day 351)
3 Where did they go to on the space tractor on Day 352?
4 Why did Captain Wells go back to the space tractor? (Day 352)
5 What did her friend decide to do, when Captain Wells did not come back quickly? (Day 352)

B Write *who* or *which* .

1 They cut small pieces from the ground, _____ was very hard.
2 Doctor Nixon, _____ stayed inside the spaceship, watched them.
3 They took three jars of liquid from the lake, _____ was yellow.
4 They put the skis on the tractor, _____ was outside the spaceship.
5 He waited for Captain Wells, _____ went to get some more film.
6 He tried to radio Doctor Nixon, _____ did not answer him.

C Put these things in the order you read about them in the passage.

| ☐ | film | ☐ | spaceship | ☐ | screens | ☐ | radio |
| 1 | microphones | ☐ | cameras | ☐ | tractor | | |

The policeman prince

1 Prince William was the son of the old king of Bavaria, in Germany, many years ago. When he was a young man, he always enjoyed adventures. This is the story of one of his adventures.

2 Prince William was staying with his family in the small town of Augsburg. The captain of the police in the town was very lazy. He was not doing his job and the people of Augsburg were becoming unhappy and angry. Their money was not safe in the banks of the town. There were a lot of thieves in the streets. Prince William heard about this and decided to make the police work harder. He had a plan.

3 One night he changed into an ordinary shirt and trousers and, with two friends, he left the king's palace late at night. The three young men went out of a door at the side of the palace. The streets were very dark because there was no moon. They did not talk.

4 They were walking down a small street when they saw two men. The two men were coming slowly and quietly down the street. They were carrying a heavy wooden box.

5 The young prince and his two friends waited quietly in the shadows. Suddenly the prince shouted 'Stop!'

6 The two men did not stop. They dropped the box and they ran, but the prince and his friends were young and strong. They could run fast. They caught the two men easily and took them both back to the palace. Inside the wooden box they found a lot of gold and silver from the biggest bank in Augsburg.

7 The next day Prince William went to see the captain of the police. The captain was sitting in his office. He was eating a pie. He jumped up quickly when he saw the prince.

8 'Have you found the gold and silver from the bank?' the prince asked. He was smiling.

9 Of course the police captain knew nothing about it. He called a few of his policemen. No, they knew nothing about

the gold from the bank. They were not very happy when the prince took them back to the palace and showed them the two thieves and the box of gold and silver.

10 They started to work harder after that and the people's money was safe inside the banks of Augsburg.

Exercises

A True or false?

1 The police captain in Augsburg always worked hard.
2 Prince William decided to help the police.
3 The two men carrying the heavy box were thieves.
4 The prince and his two friends caught the two thieves.
5 The police captain knew about the prince's plan.

B Match the words with the meanings.

dark	not young or new
lazy	usual or not special
old	sad and not happy
ordinary	not wanting to work
unhappy	with very little or no light

C Choose the right word or words.

1 The prince always (was liking / liked) an adventure.
2 The people of Augsburg (was / were) becoming unhappy and angry.
3 The two men (was / were) carrying a heavy wooden box.
4 The police captain was (eating / eaten) a pie in his office.
5 The policemen (knew / were knowing) nothing about the gold from the bank.

Tea

1 Put a little tea into a teapot. Pour some hot water into the pot. Have a cup of tea. But what is tea? Where does it come from?

5 In the high mountains of Sri Lanka, India and East Africa you can see beautiful fields of small green bushes on the hillsides. The bushes have flat tops and very bright green leaves.
10 They look like green carpets. A lot of the world's tea comes from these beautiful fields. They are called tea 'gardens'.

Every few days groups of men and
15 women, the tea-pickers, pick the leaves from the flat tops of the bushes. They only pick the youngest leaves from each tea bush. These are the leaves that make our tea. They put the
20 young leaves into baskets on their backs.

When the tea-picker's basket is full, she takes it to a lorry which will take the leaves to the tea factory. At the
25 factory, workers spread out the leaves in a large room. The leaves start to dry slowly.

They change colour from green to dark brown. After three or four days
30 the factory workers move the leaves and put them into huge machines which roll them and cut them into small pieces. The tea that we can buy in packets is in very small, dark brown
35 pieces.

There is another machine which blows wind gently through the dry, cut leaves and divides them into different sizes and grades. You can buy tea
40 which is in bigger pieces or in very small fine pieces. Pour a few of the leaves from a packet of tea onto your hand. Are the pieces of the tea-leaves quite big or are they very fine, like
45 dust?

The factory workers then pack the different grades of tea into large wooden boxes, and lorries take the

50 boxes to ships. The ships bring the tea to our different countries all over the world, and we drink it.

Exercises

A Put the sentences in order.

☐ Machines roll and cut the dry leaves into small pieces.

☐ Factory workers pack the graded tea into large wooden boxes.

☐ A lorry takes the leaves to the tea factory.

☐1 The tea-pickers pick the leaves from the bushes and put them into baskets.

☐ Workers spread out the leaves to dry for three or four days.

B Choose the best answer.

1 How do the tea-leaves go from the fields to the factory?
They go   **a** in a basket   **b** in a box   **c** in a lorry

2 How do the tea-leaves dry?
They dry   **a** in small, fine pieces   **b** slowly, on the floor   **c** in machines

3 How do the wooden boxes of tea-leaves travel to other countries?
They travel   **a** in packets   **b** in ships   **c** in factories

C Write the words in the squares.

1 Tea bushes grow in beautiful ..... on the hillsides.

2 Tea-pickers pick the leaves from the flat ..... of the bushes.

3 A tea field is called a tea '.....'.

4 It looks like a green ..... .

5 ..... bring the tea to our countries in wooden boxes.

6 The pickers put the leaves into ..... on their backs.

7 ..... take the boxes of tea to the ships.

The King of the Fish

1 'I've got *one*! Look, Otis! It's huge!'
Otis, the old fisherman, came and stood beside me at the back of the boat. We watched the huge silver fish
5 at the end of my fishing-line. *It* was jumping angrily, trying to escape.

'It's the King of the Fish! He's the biggest fish in the sea! He'll fight too,' he said quietly. He was excited.
10 The King fought hard. My arms became tired, but after two hours he was tired too and I pulled the line in slowly. We got him into the bottom of the boat and he lay there with one eye
15 open, looking at us angrily.
'He's angry,' Otis said, laughing.
He turned the boat and we went towards home. We were ten kilometres from the beach and it was
20 already evening.

Suddenly there was a loud noise: CRASH! The whole boat shook. Then there was another crash on the other side. Crash, crash, again and again. All
25 around the boat in the sea there were big silver fish. They were swimming fast, attacking our boat.
'They want their King,' the old man said. He was not laughing now.
30 'Shall we put *him* back?' I asked. I did not want to kill this beautiful big fish, the King. 'They may make a hole in the side of the boat . . .'
Otis was quiet, thinking.
35 'Yes, they may,' he answered. 'But you may never see or catch the great King of the Fish again!'
'I don't mind,' I said. 'I'm sorry for him. I want to let him go.'
40 So we lifted the King carefully and dropped him back into the sea. He lay on his side and looked up at me. He was smiling at me! Then he turned and dived down into the blue water.

45 Suddenly there were lots of silver fish in the sea round our boat. They jumped out of the waves and *they* danced. They were swimming with us now, but they did not touch the boat.

Exercises

A Answer the questions.

1 Where were the two people in this story?
2 How far away from land were they?
3 What time of day was it?
4 What attacked the sides of their boat?
5 Why did the silver fish dance around their boat?

B Read again. Answer the questions.

1 (Line 1) 'I've got *one*!' What is *one*?
2 (Line 5) '*It* was jumping . . .' What was *it*?
3 (Line 17) '*He* turned the boat . . .' Who was *he*?
4 (Line 30) 'Shall we put *him* back?' Who was *him*?
5 (Line 47) '. . . and *they* danced.' Who were *they*?

C Find words.

```
f w q p l i n e k b
c a y b e a c h v n
k v x h y w h g k f
n e z b k a f s l i
h s c l p t k e g s
g y q q k e c a p h
s i l v e r q f b q
q f i s h e r m a n
h c v k g b l u e z
b o a t f n h v c g
```

The games we play

1 Think of all the *different* games that people play: games for one player, like some card-games; games for two players, like tennis or chess; games
5 for teams, like football.

Do you have one *favourite* game that you play often with your friends? Which games do you like most?

Children have played games for
10 thousands of years. Some children's games are very old. There were swings, for example, on the Greek island of Crete about 3,600 years ago. Children in Ancient Greece played the
15 game of 'jacks' with stones, too.
Some games have become more *popular* from century to century. Other games have become less popular and have almost disappeared. For
20 example, not many people now play games that hurt or kill animals.
And people have discovered or invented new things which have changed the history of children's
25 games. Do you ever play with a ball, for example? A rubber ball? For thousands of years people played with

hard wooden or leather balls. But rubber comes out of rubber trees and
30 someone discovered this. They made new, soft balls of rubber, which bounced. Games with balls then became much more popular. Most children now have a rubber ball at
35 home.
Have you ever played with a kite? Have you got a kite at home? Kites first came from China. Travellers brought them across Asia to Europe
40 and North Africa.

Then, about four hundred years ago, people started to use games for teaching and learning in schools. There was a popular geography
45 game: the teacher cut out the shapes of countries and the children tried to put the countries in the right places again. This was the first jigsaw puzzle. Do you ever do jigsaw puzzles?
50 Now we play games like 'snakes and ladders' for learning and for enjoying ourselves. 'Snakes and ladders' has become one of the most popular games in the world.

Exercises

A **True or false?**

1 Some card-games are only for one player.
2 Children first played with 'jacks' in Crete.
3 Games which hurt animals have become more popular.
4 People played with wooden balls before they had rubber ones.
5 People first used jigsaw puzzles to learn geography.

B **Choose the best answer.**

1 'different games' (line 1) are games
  a which are all the same
  b which are not all the same
  c which are not easy
2 Your 'favourite game' (line 6) is the game
  a which you like most
  b which you like least
  c which you play last
3 A 'popular game' (line 17) is a game
  a which a lot of people like
  b which very few people like
  c which hurts animals

C **Put these games or toys in the order you read about them in the passage.**

☐ kites   ☐ snakes and ladders   ☐ rubber balls

☐ jacks   1 swings   ☐ jigsaw puzzles

☐ wooden or leather balls

Picture dictionary

a beach	bouncing	a burger	a bush	a butterfly
a camp	a canoe	a card	a carpet	a cartoon
a century	a chain-saw	chasing	escaping	chess
a cookie	a desert	dividing	diving	a donut
dust	earth	an elephant	fighting	flat

Note: 'cookie' and 'donut' are American English, in British English you use 'biscuit' and 'doughnut'.

22

fruit   a gun   a hippopotamus   a hole   a king

a kite   a laboratory   straight lines   a lion   logs

a microphone   packing   a palace   a path   a pizza

a planet   pulling   pushing   rubber   sailing

a salad   a screen   a shadow   shapes   skis

sailing   skiing

horse – riding   swimming   canoeing

sports

a studio

a summit

a swing

a team

a teapot

a tent

a tiger

a trunk

a hillside

a village

a forest

a valley